RESET

31 DAYS TO REFLECT ON, REIGNITE, AND RUN WITH YOUR FAITH

ANNA HILL MOORE

RESET© 2022 by Anna Hill Moore
All rights reserved.

Printed in the United States of America

Published by Author Academy Elite
P. O. Box 43
Powell, OH 43035

All rights reserved. No part of this publication may be reproduced, stored in a retrieval system, or transmitted in any form or by any means—for example, electronic, mechanical, photocopying, recording—without the prior written permission of the author. The only exception is in brief quotations in printed reviews.

Library of Congress Number: 2021925562
Softcover: 978-1-64746-980-1
Hardcover: 978-1-64746-981-8
E-book: 978-1-64746-982-5

Available in softcover, hardcover, e-book, and audiobook.

All scripture quotations unless otherwise indicated are taken from the Holy Bible NIV, NKJV, TLT.

DEDICATION

This book is dedicated to the memory of two persons who have left a mark on my life and the lives of countless others.

First, to the memory of Peggy Hurst Johnson, who embodied the authentic Christian walk we should all seek. She modeled love, grace, faith, exhortation, gentleness, and endurance. Peggy walked out Proverbs 31 in her daily life. She loved God with all of her heart, all of her soul, all of her strength, and all of her mind. She was, and continues to be, deeply loved by her family and friends. Her influence and impact will continue for generations through her legacy of faith. Peggy, I look forward to seeing you again in Heaven, where your faith has become sight.

Second, to the memory of James "Mike" Finger. Mike's overriding mission on this earth was to lead people to Jesus. He did this unashamedly and with no apologies. Mike loved people, and that love extended to everyone he encountered. Mike supported my writing effort at every step, offering encouragement and the occasional "When are you gonna get that book done, girl?" Mike left an imprint on this world and on my life that will never be erased. Thank you, Mike, for loving me and my family, for pushing me forward in the kingdom work, and for the prayers which have changed us all. I will be so happy to celebrate with you at the feast in heaven. Until then, let your laughter ring loud in the celestial space, where you walk without impediment and your heart is completely healed.

ACKNOWLEDGMENTS

Many thanks to my dear and patient husband, my children, my siblings, my friends, and my prayer group. The Igniting Souls community and Kary Oberbrunner became a part of my life at *just the right time*, encouraging and guiding me along this path. I am forever indebted to Faye Bryant, my friend and coach, for her leadership, oversight, and guidance with this project and so much more.

Jeff, thank you for always encouraging me to grow, to seek the path of my calling, and to look beyond today.

Linda and Mary, your constant and consistent encouragement and friendship have kept me from falling off the path. You have picked me up and challenged me all along the way.

Greater Things Ministry and Kingdom Access School have meant so much to me during this process. All those special people who know God, hear God, and love me despite knowing me, have taken me beyond what I could have ever imagined. May the Lord continue to richly bless His work in and through you all.

I love each one of you. Thank you for standing by me and for standing with me.

Most of all, thank You God, for never giving up on me. Thank You for loving me with a never-ending and unfathomable love. Thank You for accepting me just as I am. Thank You for valuing me. Thank You for Your sacrifice for me and Your gift of salvation. I am eternally Yours.

Blessings to all,

Ann

Matthew 6:33

TABLE OF CONTENTS

Introduction xi

Part One: Who Is God?

Chapter 1	The Eternal One.	3
Chapter 2	Creator	7
Chapter 3	Omnipotent.	11
Chapter 4	Omniscient	15
Chapter 5	Omnipresent	19
Chapter 6	Love	23
Chapter 7	Our Guide.	27
Chapter 8	Abba	31
Chapter 9	Redeemer	35

Part Two: Who Am I?

Chapter 10	Who am I? Beloved One	41
Chapter 11	Who am I? His Child	45

Chapter 12   Who Am I? The Work of His Hands... 49
Chapter 13   Who am I? The One in Whom
              Your Spirit Abides................. 53
Chapter 14   Who am I? The Hands
              and Feet of God 57
Chapter 15   Who am I? Warrior................ 61
Chapter 16   Who am I? His Ambassador 65

Part Three: Relationship

Chapter 17   Connection: The First Step
              with the Lord 71
Chapter 18   Communion: Deepening Intimacy
              with God......................... 75
Chapter 19   Conversation: Friendship
              with the Lord 79
Chapter 20   Conviction: Bringing my Need
              to Awareness..................... 83
Chapter 21   Confession: Agreement with the Lord.. 87
Chapter 22   Correction: Changing the Course 91
Chapter 23   Commission: His Plan for Me....... 95

Part Four: Moving Forward

Chapter 24   Step 1: Respond 101
Chapter 25   Step 2: Renew 105
Chapter 26   Step 3: Relinquish................109
Chapter 27   Step 4: Remember.................113
Chapter 28   Step 5: Release 117
Chapter 29   Step 6: Resurrect Your Passion.......121
Chapter 30   Step 7: Recreate your future.........125
Chapter 31   Step 8: Relish the Relationship 129

Afterword 133

INTRODUCTION

Hello, dear reader. Thank you so much for choosing this book to be part of your library. I pray you find what you need to reignite your faith, your passion, and your desire for a deeper walk with God.

RESET began to take shape as I drove to work on a clear winter morning in 2019. As I began to develop the manuscript, the Lord walked me through each and every step along the way. I have experienced the book for myself . . . and it changed me . . . just as I hope it changes you.

This book is written for those of us who love the Lord and want a deeper intimacy with Him. Maybe we have slacked off in our enthusiasm. Maybe we have become so busy with day-to-day life that we have neglected the most important relationship we have—the one with the Lord God Almighty.

These daily readings are designed to get us back to basics while digging a little deeper into ourselves—listening for what He has to say to us. Using what I have termed the **Pause-Ponder-Reflect** method, you will begin the day with a brief reading (Pause), you will let this meander around in your head throughout the day (Ponder), and at the end of the day, you will write out what you heard from the Lord regarding the content (Reflect).

Join me as we revisit key truths about God, about ourselves, and what our relationship with Him means. We will do all this while asking the Holy Spirit for guidance and wisdom. Each day will include a reading, a contemplation, a prayer, a corresponding scripture, and a declaration.

Please begin each reading in prayer that the Lord will lead you to what He has for you that day. Be open and expectant to hear from Him. He says we will find Him when we seek Him with all of our heart.

PART ONE
WHO IS GOD?

DAY 1
THE ETERNAL ONE

In the beginning, God . . .

God. Present before time. Will be present long after time has stopped.

One God.

As human beings, finite creatures, we live our lives based on *Time*. Time is not merely a concept. Time is abstract yet concrete. It is abstract in that we cannot *see* time . . . yet concrete in that we have ways to measure it. The rising and setting of the sun marks our days. Changes in the environment mark our seasons. Both are measures of time. We have clocks, watches, and timers on our phones and appliances, which provide even more ways to measure time. In a way, the growth we see in our children and the aging we see in ourselves also marks the passing of time . . .

God created time when he created all that came into existence.

In the beginning . . . Genesis 1:1 . . . God

God began time. He chose the moment when it would start, like the person who shoots the starting pistol at a road race. God said simply, "Now," and it was done.

Our first introduction to God is as the *Eternal One*.

Today, let's wrap our little minds around that truth: *God is eternal*.

Contemplation: Sit for a few minutes pondering the truth that God is the Eternal One. You may not be able to fully comprehend all that it means, but let that truth seep into the crevices of your heart and mind. Allow it to permeate every fiber of your being without asking questions. Questions can come later. For now, just let the truth that He is Eternal wash over you.

Prayer: Lord, pierce my heart today with the truth that You are the Eternal God.

1 Timothy 1:17 NIV

Now to the King eternal, immortal, invisible, the only God, be honor and glory forever and ever. Amen.

DECLARATION

I declare that God is eternal, and that He is outside of time and space. Although my finite mind cannot completely grasp it, I accept it as truth.

REFLECTION:

DAY 2
CREATOR

God

Eternal

Creator

God is the CREATOR.

God created the heavens and earth. They were formed from nothing. All the elements that exist today were created at this point in time.

After forming the heavens and the earth, a perfect, but empty creation, His Spirit hovered over the vastness of the earth. Then He spoke and began to implement His Grand Design.

Because of His word—the spoken word of the triune God, Elohim.

"Let there be . . ."

Light

Sky

Water

Plants

Sun, Moon, and Stars

Birds and Aquatic life

Land animals

Mankind . . . created in the image of God—in the image of the triune God—was created with a body, soul, and spirit. The very breath of God was breathed into His most beloved creation. Mankind was given authority over the earth and everything in it. Freedom to choose was granted to them.

Man was created from the dust of the ground . . . from the very elements that God had spoken into being.

Imagine God reaching down into the dust. Imagine Him making clay and sculpting man. The Great Potter creating a unique piece of art . . .

Then woman was created from the rib of man . . . the one God had already created.

Everything that is in existence is a result of God's Creation.

And God saw that His Creation was good, and He rested.

Contemplation: Look around you. What do you see? Notice all of God's Creation. Be aware of His Creation as you move throughout your day. Let Him show you the intricacies you have never before noticed.

Prayer: Lord, renew a sense of awe in me today as I look on your Creation, realizing that I, too, am a result of your handiwork.

Isaiah 40:28 NIV

Do you not know? Have you not heard? The Lord is the everlasting God, the Creator of the ends of the earth.

DECLARATION

Today I declare that I am the product of God the Creator. He continues His work of creation and transformation in me. He sees me and says that I am good. I am His work of art, His masterpiece.

REFLECTION:

DAY 3
OMNIPOTENT

God is Omnipotent

Omnipotent = All Powerful

God is All Powerful.

All. Not some. Not partially. Not 75%. Not 99.9% . . .

All powerful.

This characteristic of God is first displayed in His Creation. The very fact that He created the heavens and the earth demonstrates His great power.

Throughout the Bible, His power continued to be shown. The parting of the Red Sea stands out as a mighty demonstration of His ability to affect the natural order of things. He delivered the children of Israel after showing Himself through the plagues. He then showed Himself as a cloud in the day and a pillar of fire at night. He spoke to Moses on the mountain with displays of thunder and lightning. When He was in the tabernacle, a cloud filled it. The Israelites knew it to be Him and they were afraid. Why? Because of the display of His great power.

These were very public demonstrations of His power.

In the Old Testament, He raised up kings and warriors, and gave them victory by His word. The walls of Jericho fell at His command.

He fed a widow and her son by providing an unending supply of oil and flour as they housed a prophet.

He raised the dead. This happened through the prophets in the Old Testament and through Jesus in the New Testament.

We see Jesus turn water into wine, feed the multitudes, walk on water, heal the sick, cast out demons, calm the storm, and raise the dead.

Then Jesus, the very physical manifestation of God on earth, defeats death and rises from the dead after three days.

This is the ultimate display of His power.

But perhaps the capstone display of His Omnipotence goes beyond His resurrection. Perhaps it is truly seen in His ability to change an individual's heart. In His ability to change the inner self.

His gift of Salvation, received and applied in a life, is the conclusive display of His omnipotence. Why? Because He doesn't just save us from death. He saves us *from ourselves*.

Contemplation: Look around you. Where do you see God's power displayed today? Ask Him to show you, then look and listen.

Prayer: Lord, show me Your power today.

Colossians 1:17 NIV

He is before all things, and in Him all things hold together.

DECLARATION

I declare that the all-powerful Lord God is at work in my life today for His glory and my good.

REFLECTION:

DAY 4
OMNISCIENT

God is Omniscient.

God knows everything.

Everything.

Past, present, future.

About me. About you. About everything.

The Eternal Creator, the omnipotent God knew from the beginning how the human story was going to go down. He knew how temptation, sin, and rejection would play out.

He knew the pain that would come. The pain it would cause Him. The pain it would cause us.

He knew the big picture as well as the minute details of each individual life.

He also knew His plan for love, forgiveness, and redemption with all that would entail. The hardships and the victories. The rejection, denial, abuse, and murder of His only son.

He knew... but despite the knowing, He did not give up on us, throw us away, or deny us. He continued to let His plan work.

He continues to allow us free will to choose our way in this life. To allow us to make our own decisions and to live with the consequences of those decisions.

He wants us to come to Him, to rest in Him, to choose Him above all else.

Always He loves us, with an everlasting love. He is not fickle as humans can be.

He knows how we feel, what we think, and what our motivations are. He knows things about us that we don't know about ourselves.

Yet He continues to pursue us, to woo us, to wait for us to respond.

He knows all, but He loves us and values us anyway.

God is Omniscient.

Contemplation: What does God know about you that no one else knows? Ponder how much He loves you and pursues you regardless of this.

Prayer: Lord, thank You for loving me despite knowing me fully.

Genesis 16:13 NIV

She gave this name to the Lord who spoke to her, "You are the God who sees me"

DECLARATION

I declare today that God—who knows every detail about me—loves everything about me, and that His love is never-ending. There is no shame in His presence—only Love.

REFLECTION:

DAY 5
OMNIPRESENT

God is Omnipresent. He is everywhere.

He is Spirit, transcending time and space.

Regardless of where I am, He is there. He is here as I write. He is present as I walk in the woods. He is with me when I sleep.

Although I may not sense Him (see, hear, feel, taste, or touch Him), He nevertheless is present in every moment and every circumstance.

He was present in my past and will be present in my future.

This does not frighten me. Instead, it comforts me.

This should not shame me. When I have behaved in ways contrary to His character or been in places or situations that would displease Him, His presence was also there. Rather than shame, I should feel His unconditional love for me.

Why? Because nothing surprises Him. He is omniscient and omnipresent.

His omnipresence may be a deterrent for my willful sin, but often I fail to recognize or acknowledge that He is with me.

Contemplation: Think about God being with you now, wherever you are. Consider His constant presence as you move through your day today.

Prayer: Lord God, open our hearts and minds to an awareness of Your constant presence, so that we may fellowship with You, the one true God, the lover and keeper of our souls and spirits.

Jeremiah 23:24 NIV

"Who can hide in secret places so that I cannot see them?" declares the Lord. "Do I not fill heaven and earth?" declares the Lord.

DECLARATION

I declare that God is with me always, just as Jesus said He would be. His presence with me is a comfort on this great adventure. He is my best friend. We are going places together, and He will never leave me or forsake me. He is always dependable. He is trustworthy. He is God.

REFLECTION:

_____
_____
_____
_____
_____
_____
_____
_____
_____
_____
_____
_____

DAY 6
LOVE

God is Love

God. Is. Love.

Love . . . what is your definition? What do you think of when you think of love?

Have you experienced love? Or has your life been devoid of love?

The word love is used in a variety of contexts. We say we love a movie, a performer, a song, a food . . .

We say we love our children, parents, teachers, friends . . .

We say we "love it when" and fill in the blank however we desire . . .

But do we really know what love is? We think we do, but often our perception of love is based on our personal experiences, our cultural training, and what the entertainment industry portrays as love.

Therefore, we have an incomplete understanding and a skewed perception of love. We think of it as a feeling that we experience . . . but feelings come and go, and love is so much more . . .

When it comes to love, God has it all. He is not only the source of love, He *is* love.

Think back for a moment to a time when you felt love. Focus on that moment. Hold it carefully and sacredly in your mind's eye. Do not allow any other thoughts to come in—just experience it again.

As you hold that moment, allow God to join you, to stand beside you. See Him with you in that moment, smiling, His hand on your shoulder, taking pleasure in your moment of love. See Him looking into your eyes as you smile at each other, experiencing this moment together.

As the author and the source of love, God takes great pleasure when you experience love.

He wants you to know love because He wants you to know Him.

These earthly tastes of divine love whet our appetite for the true and deeper love of our Father God.

If your life has been devoid of love, you can know it when you know Him. As His creation, our spirits seek love. Our desire for love is rooted in the source of our creation: God. We are drawn to love because we are drawn to Him. He is always drawing us back to Himself.

Contemplation: God is love. He is beyond any past love that I have experienced. He loves me unconditionally—no strings attached. His love is eternal. He does not love me only to withdraw His love when I displease Him. He loves because He *is*. And because He is Love.

God Is Love.

Prayer: Lord God, help me to begin to understand the depth of Your love for me.

1 John 4:8 NIV

Whoever does not love does not know God, because God is love.

DECLARATION

I declare today that I am eternally and unconditionally loved by God—who is the source of love. I open my hands and my heart to receive that love from the one who is Love. This pure love flows directly from His heart to mine, requiring only my acceptance of it.

REFLECTION:

DAY 7
OUR GUIDE

God is our guide.

God—the eternal creator—is our guide through all of life. He prepares each path we take with signposts in plain sight. Yet how can we see or hear His directions if we are disconnected? We stumble through life blind to Him, deaf to His voice—as if someone pulled out the audio and visual feeds from a television. We are left with only silence and darkness.

But when we are connected, when we have the "feed" from the Father via the Holy Spirit—our path is clear—it is brightly lit, with every step we need to see. Even Jesus could do only what the Father directed.

How did Jesus know what to do? He maintained His relationship with God. He pulled away from the crowds to be alone with the Father, to hear from Him.

Jesus heard from the Father, then moved in obedience. God is our guide, but it is our responsibility to follow . . .

Contemplation: Are you accessing the Holy Spirit "feed" for your life? Or are you disconnected?

Prayer: Lord, make Your path clear to me today. I want to experience the leadership of your Holy Spirit in my life.

John 14:26 NIV

But the Advocate, the Holy Spirit, whom the Father will send in my name, will teach you all things and will remind you of everything I have said to you.

DECLARATION

Today I declare that God is my guide. I have eyes to see Him, ears to hear His voice, and feet to follow Him. I will seek to experience Him as a I travel throughout my day.

REFLECTION:

DAY 8
ABBA

God is Abba—Father.

Abba knows me intimately.

Abba knew me before He formed me in my mother's womb.

Abba is familiar with the intricacies of my body, my heart, my spirit—because He created me and made me just the way He wanted me to be.

Abba holds me when I am fearful.

Abba disciplines me when I need it.

Abba leads me on this path we call life.

And when I address Him as Abba, it is with the respect of a dearly beloved child and the reverence accorded to the King of Kings and Lord of Lords.

While I take none of this for granted, I am aware of Abba's deep and abiding love.

I am aware of His deep knowing of me and I cherish the intimacy of our relationship.

Abba . . . Father . . . Eternal God . . . the Creator of the universe . . . loves me and wants me as His child. He invites me to His throne to be with Him and talk to Him.

Abba loves me.

I am His . . . and He is mine.

Contemplation: Visualize yourself knocking on the door or ringing the doorbell of the house where God lives. Imagine Him inviting you in to sit for a while, on a comfy couch in the living room or at the table in the kitchen. Offering you a cup of coffee, hot chocolate, or tea. Be at home with your Abba Father today. Enjoy being in His presence. He loves you so much.

Prayer: Abba Father, let me know Your love and fondness for me today. Let me enjoy time with You.

Romans 8: 15 NIV

The Spirit you received does not make you slaves so that you live in fear again; rather, the Spirit you received brought about your adoption to sonship. And by Him we cry "Abba, Father."

DECLARATION

I declare that the King of Kings and Lord of Lords is my daddy. Abba delights in me and invites me to abide in His presence. He is proud to call me His child. We make a great family.

REFLECTION:

DAY 9
REDEEMER

God is the Redeemer.

The Eternal Creator who is omniscient, omnipotent, and omnipresent is the Redeemer.

The Redeemer. The One and Only Redeemer.

He came to earth as a man, whose name was Jesus, with a singular purpose—to become our Redeemer.

During His life—and pilgrimage to the cross—He loved, taught, and performed many miracles. Yet His ultimate destination was always the cross.

Only by laying down His life—His sinless life—could He become the final sacrifice for the sins of mankind.

Contemplation: Jesus's mission on earth was to live so that He could die, fulfilling God's Word. He died so we can live.

Prayer: Father, remind me of Your sacrifice. Your sacrifice was necessary to redeem me.

John 15:13 NIV

Greater love has no one than this: to lay down one's life for one's friends.

DECLARATION

I declare that Jesus Christ is the one and only Redeemer, who lived to die so that I may live. I know that my Redeemer lives. I will rejoice in the gift of His sacrifice for me. I will rest in His completed work.

REFLECTION:

PART TWO
WHO AM I?

DAY 10
WHO AM I? BELOVED ONE

I am His Beloved One.

I am the one who He loves.

In fact, He not only calls me the one who He loves, but calls me His Beloved. Oh, the warmth, radiance, and security that name carries!

The Beloved One of the Most High God . . .

The Beloved One of the Eternal Creator, the Lord of Heaven and Earth.

The Beloved One of the Redeemer, the Father, the Spirit.

I am—you are—His Beloved One.

His Beloved One.

Cherished

Desired

Admired

Pursued

Rescued

Restored

Delighted In

Your "beloved" status includes all these descriptions.

Oh, precious, beloved one! Can you sense His deep and abiding love? Can you feel His presence? Can you feel joy begin to bubble up inside your chest, until it overflows and encompasses you?

The love of God pouring into His Beloved will change everything.

Receive it.

Contemplation: Imagine a fountain of love pouring forth from the throne of Heaven into your heart. You are His Beloved One.

Prayer: Lord, open my heart and help me to receive the awareness that I am Your Beloved One.

1 John 4:7 NKJV

Beloved, let us love one another, for love is of God; and everyone who loves is born of God and knows God.

DECLARATION

I declare that I am His Beloved One. His love is pouring out over me and into my life. I open my hands, my heart, and my spirit to receive it now.

REFLECTION:

DAY 11
WHO AM I? HIS CHILD

God calls me His Child.

He formed me in my mother's womb.

He thought about me before time began.

He knows every day—every detail of my life—past, present, and future.

He asks me to call Him Father.

And like a good father, He loves me. He provides for me, He protects me, and He is available for me.

He sees my tears, and His heart aches for me.

He sees my successes, and His heart rejoices for me!

He is always at work in the background of my life, carefully preparing the way so my path is clear.

The obstacles that He allows along the way serve to teach me the life lessons that come only from experience. This strengthens my trust and endurance.

All the while He is nearby, watching over me as I move along the path. He is there—ready to help—ready with the answer I need at that very moment.

I am like a toddler, unable to see over my current obstacle. He is like a tall, strong Father who sees me and my path from a higher vantage point. He sees clearly all the obstacles, the depths of my struggle, and the path beyond.

He encourages me to keep moving forward, keep climbing, and never look back.

Each challenge becomes bigger as I continue to grow in Him, but my fear lessens the further I travel along the path—because I have learned to trust my Father.

He calls me "Child."

Contemplation: Are you like a toddler with the Father, following your own whims and distractions? Or are you learning to follow His voice and direction for your best path?

Prayer: Lord, I love knowing that I am Your child and that You never give up on me. Help me to learn to listen to You and to trust You with all my days.

Galatians 4:7 NIV

You are no longer a slave, but God's child; and since you are His child, God has also made you also an heir.

DECLARATION

I declare that I am a beloved child of God. My Father knows me, loves me, and rejoices in our relationship. I will walk in my identity as a royal child of the Most High King.

REFLECTION:

DAY 12
WHO AM I? THE WORK OF HIS HANDS

I am the Work of His Hands.

After all of creation was completed—by Your very Word, Lord—You reached down with Your hands and formed the first man. You could have spoken Adam into existence, but instead you chose to get your heavenly hands dirty, reaching down into the very dirt that You had already spoken into existence. You carefully, thoughtfully, and with great precision formed a creature unlike any of the others.

This creature would be Your image-bearer and would be commissioned to oversee the rest of Your creation.

You formed Adam, then You breathed Your holy breath into his lungs, giving him a life and a soul like none before him.

Created to display Your glory, as is all of Creation, humankind was uniquely gifted with a soul and a longing for connection with You, the Creator.

And from that first man came the entire human race. Even today, You continue Your "hands on" creation of humans as You knit them together in their mothers' wombs.

I am—we are—the Work of Your Hands.

Contemplation: Consider the intricacies and individuality of every single human on earth. We are all different because He has made us so. How has He made you different from others?

Prayer: Lord, help me to understand the uniqueness of Your design in me, not to be boastful or proud, but to acknowledge Your great commissioning of each individual.

Psalm 139:13 NIV

For you created my inmost being; you knit me together in my mother's womb.

DECLARATION

I declare that I am a unique creation of God, made just the way He planned. I am like no other human who has come before or who will come after. He made me by the work of His hands.

REFLECTION:

DAY 13
WHO AM I? THE ONE IN WHOM YOUR SPIRIT ABIDES

I am the one in whom Your Spirit abides.

We are together now. As Your child, I carry You with me. We will always be together.

Your Spirit abides in and with me. Since the moment of my spiritual "conception," You made Your dwelling place in my heart.

As I grow and mature in my spiritual walk, I begin to know You and Your presence better. I experience the world through Your eyes as You make Yourself known to me.

Just as a little child who sees things from a different physical perspective than their parents, I can only see from my immature spiritual perspective until You lift me high and show me. I still cannot comprehend the extent of Your work. Even when You show me, I cannot fully understand because I am human. Until I am spiritually mature enough to understand Your teachings, I must simply walk forward, trusting You.

Holding on to You as a small child would hold the hands of their parents . . . safe from harm, happily engaged in life, and full of faith . . . let me walk through life with You.

With Your Spirit leading as an internal and external guide, my days are destined to be worthwhile, meaningful, and impactful.

Don't let me pull away from Your grasp as a small child might. Hold me steady, Lord, and let me feel and know the presence of Your abiding Spirit!

I am the one in whom Your Spirit dwells.

What a privilege! That You would choose me—choose *my* heart—in which to abide!

Contemplation: How does knowing that God abides in you make you feel?

Prayer: Lord, help me to become even more aware of Your abiding Spirit in me. When outside influences pull me away, let me hear Your quiet voice calling me back to You. Help me to make You the center and focus of my universe—the one and only God.

Romans 8:11 NIV

And if the Spirit of Him who raised Jesus from the dead is living in you He who raised Christ from the dead will also give life to your mortal bodies because of his Spirit who lives in you.

DECLARATION

I declare that the Spirit of the Living God abides in me. This is the same Spirit that raised Jesus from the dead, the comforter and teacher He promised. Therefore, I have nothing to fear.

REFLECTION:

DAY 14
WHO AM I? THE HANDS AND FEET OF GOD

I am the hands and feet of God.

Hands that "do." Feet that "go."

The Lord God Almighty dwells *with* and *in* me. I am the instrument through which His will is carried out. This human body reveals Him to the world. As His indwelling Spirit leads, my hands and feet can "go" and "do"—but only if my own spirit agrees with Him and is willing.

God, although all-powerful and indwelling, will not force me. He will never force me. He will show me, invite me, woo me, and love me. He will speak gently to me. He will instruct me. However, the choice is ultimately mine to be His hands and feet—to be the "physical manifestation" of Him to the world around me.

If only I would live so that He is what the world sees when they look at me . . .

If only I would fully rest in the reality of the one and only God of the universe who is in me . . .

If only I would remember that the very power that raised Jesus from the dead is in me now—a power like no other . . .

Contemplation: What would it look like for you to be His hands and feet today?

Prayer: Lord, let me be Your hands and feet today. Let me put myself aside and focus on the things You focus on. Let me live my human life in Your power and strength—You, the one and only Eternal God, Creator of Heaven and Earth, and Fulfiller of Dreams.

Ephesians 2:10 NIV

For we are God's handiwork, created in Christ Jesus to do good works, which God prepared in advance for us to do.

DECLARATION

The Spirit that dwells in me is the same Spirit that raised Christ from the dead. I will walk in the strength of the Holy Spirit as I follow the Lord's direction and obey Jesus's command to "go."
He will be displayed and will receive the glory. I am becoming more like Him with every step.

REFLECTION:

DAY 15
WHO AM I? WARRIOR

I am a warrior.

I am training for battle in the spiritual realm, and I know that my God is already the victor.

The skirmishes that occur along this road we call life are just that—minor skirmishes—for He has won the war over death. The outcome is sure, and when time is complete, evil will be no more.

But these skirmishes, these ongoing battles, often engage our whole persons. While unable to pluck us from His hand, the evil one longs to break our communion with our Heavenly Father. He wants to weaken us and make us ineffective soldiers for the kingdom.

But God . . .

God says:

I've got this.

I've got you.

Just hold on to Me.

Trust Me,

And prepare yourself,

For you are My warrior.

"Every battle is won in prayer, so pray, child, pray. Come to Me, bring it all to Me, and I will show you the battle plan."

As a warrior, I must be constantly in training with my team—my company—my squadron. Those like-minded believers who surround me, by the grace of God, are my people. He placed them in my life to give me strength, support, and guidance.

We train by sharing the Word with each other, by being in fellowship with our church family, and by hearing the preaching and teaching of God's Scripture. We train as we pray together and see the hand of God at work in each other's lives.

I am a warrior, and I will gird myself with the holy armor of God. I will stand on the truth of His Word and surround myself with my tribe of believers. I will listen to and hear the Lord God Almighty—the Commander of angel armies—as He directs my daily battle plan.

My battlefield will be at the feet of the One who loves me more than anyone else. I will battle in prayer for the lives of those around me, for the souls of the unsaved, and for the future yet to come.

I am a warrior.

Contemplation: What does being a warrior in His army look like to you?

Prayer: Lord, show me how I am to walk out my calling to be Your warrior. Lord, give me the strength to keep moving forward. Give me the confidence in *You*, not in myself, so I may live my life as You would have me live.

Ephesians 6:11 NIV

Put on the full armor of God, so that you can take your stand against the devil's schemes.

DECLARATION

I serve in the army of the Living God who goes before me, walks with me, and comes behind me in every circumstance. The battle is His, and I am His instrument. I will battle with the weapons of prayer, praise, and worship. My eyes will remain on my commander, the Lord of angel armies.
He cannot fail.

REFLECTION:

DAY 16
WHO AM I? HIS AMBASSADOR

I am His Ambassador.

I represent Him to the world.

When the world sees me, they see Him.

They see me—a mere human—with all my failures, achievements, and flaws. The world judges me on what they see. It is human nature.

But when they know I am His, the judgment goes deeper, and they begin to judge Him as well. Even though the world may not say it, they are looking beyond me to the One who I profess as my God.

And if the word judgment sounds too harsh, we may use the word "opinion." The world's opinion of God is formed by what they see in the lives of believers.

Am I kind, gentle, faithful?

Am I true?

Do others see the love of Jesus in me?

Or am I self-centered? Uncaring? Harsh?

Am I ruled by my humanity? Or am I led by my spiritual Father?

Do I put on a good show for the world because I think I am supposed to behave a certain way? Or have I allowed Him to really transform my inner being?

After all, I am His Ambassador.

Contemplation: Who is on display in your life?

Prayer: As I walk with You in the truth of Your Word, may I be transformed so that only You are seen, Lord.

2 Corinthians 5:20a NIV

We are therefore Christ's ambassadors, as though God were making an appeal through us.

DECLARATION

I will serve as the Lord's Ambassador to the world. I will bring honor to His name as I represent Him to those around me. Others will be drawn to Him as they see His love and goodness represented in me.

REFLECTION:

PART THREE
RELATIONSHIP

DAY 17
CONNECTION: THE FIRST STEP WITH THE LORD

What are the first steps in any relationship? We are just getting to know each other—again, or perhaps for the very first time. How do we start?

We meet.

We are introduced, and over time, we begin to connect.

We get together and learn the basics about each other. We begin to test each other and trust each other. This is how it works for humans.

But with God? He already knows us—and He longs for that connection. In fact, He is just waiting for us to respond to His invitation to get to know Him better.

Today as you reflect on who God is and who you are, take a few moments to quietly connect with Him. Establish some time to spend alone with Him, open to His Spirit. Push aside all your thoughts and cares—they will still be there afterward.

Invite Him to join you, to show you something new about Himself. Ask Him to open your senses to His presence, then wait expectantly, because He will come.

Today as you connect with Him, contemplate the faithfulness of God.

If you are truly seeking Him with a sincere heart, you can be assured He will always show up when invited—because He is faithful.

And after He has revealed Himself to you today, when you have connected with Him, write down your experience. This is only the beginning of a beautiful journey . . .

Contemplation: Think about the faithfulness of God as you spend time with Him today. What are some ways He has shown Himself to be faithful to you?

Prayer: Lord, thank You for Your faithfulness to me, Your child. Continue to make me aware of it as we navigate this life together.

1 Corinthians 1:9 NIV

God is faithful, who has called you into fellowship with his Son, Jesus Christ our Lord.

DECLARATION

I declare that God is the faithful lover of my soul. The Lord God of the Universe has His eye on me. He has marked me as His chosen companion and friend.

REFLECTION:

DAY 18
COMMUNION: DEEPENING INTIMACY WITH GOD

The Oxford dictionary defines communion as "the sharing or exchanging of intimate thoughts or feelings, especially when the exchange is on a mental or spiritual level."

Communion takes our experience of God to a new and deeper level. It is, by its very nature, intimate. Once we have learned to connect, we have the *option* to commune.

Many of us, as Christians, have maintained a connection, but we have not moved our relationship to the level of communion.

Imagine walking alongside a stream on a well-worn path. It is not a strenuous hike—more like a meandering stroll. The woods around you are teeming with life, but no other human is in sight. You feel a sense of peace and safety as you walk along the path.

You are not alone. The Lord is with you. Jesus walks beside you on the path. As you continue to walk along, you feel a deep sense of satisfaction and contentment. You comment on the beauty of the stream and the woods around you.

You are just walking together, enjoying the experience and each other's company, taking in the sights and sounds.

You are communing with God, just as Adam and Eve did in the garden. Spending this time alone with God—getting to know each other on a much deeper level than before.

It is being *known*—well and deeply—and loved unconditionally by God.

The sense of love, peace and acceptance brings an equilibrium.

As you commune with Him in these moments, leave your expectations behind. Just enjoy being in His presence.

Contemplation: Communion with God can occur at any moment in time because He is always with you. However, it is best enjoyed when you are alone. Look for a moment today to spend some time just being with Him.

Prayer: Lord, let me recognize Your abiding presence in my life and let me enjoy the moments of communion with You more and more as every day passes.

Psalm 139:7–8 NIV

Where can I go from your Spirit? Where can I flee from your presence? If I go up to the heavens, you are there; if I make my bed in the depths, you are there.

DECLARATION

I declare that I will walk in close communion with my Lord. I will be drawn into His deep love and abiding presence, sharing these moments of life together. I will know Him more and more with each passing day. Nothing can separate us.

REFLECTION:

DAY 19
CONVERSATION: FRIENDSHIP WITH THE LORD

Conversation with the Lord God Almighty may seem daunting at first. After all, as the psalmist writes, who are we that HE would be mindful of us? But as we have come to realize, we are so much more to Him.

We are His children, loved unconditionally. We have the indwelling of the Holy Spirit—the very Spirit of God dwells in the believer. The better we know Him, the easier it is to hear from Him.

We find talking so much easier than listening. We've learned to "pray," often speaking our praise and requests aloud or in our mind, but have we learned to *listen*?

Healthy communication between two persons is a two-way street. It involves both speaking and listening. It should be the same as we communicate with God.

We are free to speak. Encouraged to speak. We need to speak.

But we also need to listen.

Listening involves attention and focus. When God speaks, it may not be in an audible voice. It may be a pricking of your heart or a quickening in your spirit. Developing a habit of listening takes time and practice.

Just as you would sit quietly with a good friend, sharing and listening, practice sitting quietly with God.

Invite Him into your quiet place. Worship Him. Commune with Him. Talk to Him. Then sit quietly with your focus on Him and hearing Him.

Do you sense His presence? Do you feel His love? Are you quiet and completely focused on Him?

Take time to invest in your relationship with the Lord God Almighty.

As you invest your time, effort, and spirit, your listening skills will improve. Hearing will come easier.

Come to Him with expectation. Sit at the feet of the Father for a while.

When we primarily feed ourselves with the things of this world, our relationship with Him suffers. The distance between us and Him seems farther and our ability to hear declines.

If there is too much "clutter" between you and God, the "sounds" cannot penetrate.

Clear the path today—even if only for a few moments.

As you practice listening, remember that He is right there with you—accessible if you lose your concentration for a moment.

He is a good friend.

Contemplation: You can hear Him when you listen. Have you been listening? Listen today.

Prayer: Lord, help me to develop good spiritual ears so that I may hear You clearly.

Isaiah 28:23 NIV

Listen and hear my voice; pay attention and hear what I say.

DECLARATION

I declare that I will have meaningful conversation with my God. I will quiet my mind and spirit, and I will listen. He will speak. He is my shepherd. I know His voice. We are friends.

REFLECTION:

DAY 20
CONVICTION: BRINGING MY NEED TO AWARENESS

He gets my attention by gently pointing out the wrong. There is no condemnation in His approach. Instead, He lovingly illuminates the offense.

Whether it's an attitude, action, omission, or persistent focus on something that does not honor God—my God loves me enough to bring it to my attention.

As He brings it to my attention, my spirit responds with recognition. I **know** what I have allowed in my spirit that is at odds with my Lord's character.

This is called conviction. Conviction is the realization or awareness of an act, omission, or thought process that is contrary to the precepts of God. This is His way of letting us know what needs to change to move us more toward being like Christ.

The word conviction has an unpleasant connotation. To the world, conviction brings to mind guilt and subsequent punishment. However, in God's world—the world of the Spirit—conviction is not negative. In fact, it is lifegiving. It may seem unexpected to hear that conviction can be a blessing. But it becomes clear when we realize that God doesn't convict us to punish us. He convicts us to show us how to be more like Him, and to show His love toward us.

Contemplation: The Spirit of God convicts us because of His great love for us. Conviction is not condemnation. Conviction is not to be feared. What are you hearing from God today? What is He pointing out in your life that needs to change?

Prayer: Lord, show me what I need to change to be more like You. Thank You for loving me so much that You point out what is holding me back from being all You desire for me.

Psalms 51:4 NIV

Against you, you only, have I sinned and done what is evil in your sight; so you are right in your verdict and justified when you judge.

DECLARATION

I declare that I am becoming more like Christ every day. Because of His great love, I have no fear. I anticipate and eagerly seek transformation to His likeness.
Therefore, I will ask the Lord, "What would You say to me today? Your servant is listening."

REFLECTION:

DAY 21
CONFESSION: AGREEMENT WITH THE LORD

It's true, Lord. What You have revealed to me, about me, it's all true.

I fought You about it for a while. I ignored Your subtle nudge about it in my heart and spirit. I justified it, especially when I compared myself to others in the world. Nevertheless, no amount of logic can change the truth that I am wrong, and You are right.

Please hear my confession.

What a glorious thing it is that we can confess our wrongs—our sins—directly to the Lord God Almighty! That when we come to Him with our confession, He is "**faithful** and **just** to forgive."

He is faithful means you can count on Him. There is no doubt that He will do as He has promised.

He is just. He only does what is morally right and fair. The Oxford dictionary defines the word *just* as "unbiased, impartial, objective, and nondiscriminating." God is all this and more.

The Greek word for *just* is *dikaios*, meaning "righteous, observing divine laws, and rendering to each his due." What does that mean exactly? It means He sees it, judges it as sin, but pours out forgiveness instead of retribution.

Remember, confession is agreement with God that benefits only you. Unconfessed sin creates bondage and holds you captive, but confessed sin and repentance bring freedom.

Contemplation: What is one thing God has brought to mind that you need to agree with Him about? Walk in the freedom of confessing it today.

Prayer: Lord, make it clear to me, whether it is an attitude, an action, or an inaction. Whatever You need to bring to my mind today, make it clear. Give me a heart ready to confess and move forward.

1 John 1:9 NIV

If we confess our sins, he is faithful and just and will forgive us our sins and purify us from all sin.

DECLARATION

I declare that forgiveness is mine as I confess my sins to the One who offers His righteousness to me. I receive His cleansing and become more like Him in the process.

REFLECTION:

DAY 22
CORRECTION: CHANGING THE COURSE

Recognition of my wrongdoing, of "missing the mark," is the initial step. Confession is the second step and is an act of the will. I may recognize that I have done something wrong. Maybe I displayed the wrong attitude, focused on the wrong subject, or didn't do the right thing in a difficult situation . . .

But confession—admitting my wrongs—takes it a step beyond recognition. It makes it a "public" matter—public between me and God. That means I no longer harbor any illusion that He is unaware or doesn't care. I know that He knows, but if I don't talk to Him about it, I feel I don't have to deal with it. I don't have to take corrective action.

Once we have had a conversation, and I have admitted my wrongdoing, the next step is to correct that wrong.

Correction may be as simple as changing my thoughts, or it may be as complex as going to someone who I have wronged and repairing that wrong.

It is here that I need the Holy Spirit to guide me. Correcting the wrong I have done is something that I want to get right. I desire and need a renewal of my mind and a cleansing of my spirit to move forward. For until this is done, there is a gap in my fellowship with the Lord. Our friendship cannot be as sweet, and my potential cannot be fulfilled until I change my course. Only then can my heart, mind, and soul be once again at peace.

We are always moving toward a better relationship with Him.

Contemplation: How is the Father leading you to correct your confession? Ask Him today. Do not assume that you have the right answer.

Prayer: Father, You have been faithful to point out what needed confession in my life. Now, Lord, lead me in how to best correct it. I want to stay on course with You and with Your plan for me.

Psalms 51:10 NIV

Create in me a pure heart, O God, and renew a steadfast spirit within me.

DECLARATION

I declare that I will move forward on my corrected course as the Father reveals it. His way—only His way—is the desire of my heart.

REFLECTION:

DAY 23
COMMISSION: HIS PLAN FOR ME

Our relationship is deepening as we move along this path together. As I have connected, communed, and conversed with God, I have come to know Him on a deeper level. I have learned that He is loving, faithful, and trustworthy. That His interest in me is altruistic—He neither wants nor needs anything from me. There is nothing I can give Him that He doesn't already have. He is complete already.

He desires the best for me. Because of His love, I can accept the loving spirit of conviction, fearlessly speak my confession, and confidently apply the correction . . . all because I know Him, and I know that His plans and desires for me are much better than anything I could imagine on my own.

His plan is my Commission.

The Great Commission calls for us to go out into the world, teaching the world about Jesus, baptizing believers, and making new disciples. (see Matthew 28:18-20)

It is obvious that we are not all called to be missionaries on foreign fields, but we are all called to do something. We are all on a "co-mission" with the Lord. Wherever we find ourselves, we are to be sharing Jesus and making disciples.

How exactly that plays out looks different for each of us. You must ask the One who created you exactly how you are to carry out your commission. Regardless of where the Lord has placed you, you *are* commissioned.

While we all have a part in the overall commission—sharing the gospel and making disciples—God has a specific and individual purpose for each of us. By growing in our intimacy with Him, we will discover our personal call. One person may be called to full-time ministry or mission work, another may be called to work in the secular world, while another may be called to be a stay-at-home parent. Whatever He calls you to is your call—not your mother's, father's, husband's, or wife's call. While He may call you to partner with someone, your call is still *your* call. Wherever you are, you bring the Kingdom with you. Living by Kingdom principles will speak to those around you in ways that words cannot. God's work, wherever He places you, is a holy work because you are His holy child.

If having a call on your life makes you anxious or fearful, remember that God is the source of your strength. He provides what you need to fulfill your call. Lean close into Him and He will direct your paths.

Contemplation: Think about where He has placed you right now. How can you carry out your commission right where you are?

Prayer: Lord, show me the commission You have for my life. Give me the strength and knowledge to live out Your calling for me in my day-to-day life.

Psalms 23: 3 NIV

He refreshes my soul. He guides me along the right paths for His name's sake.

DECLARATION

I declare that I am commissioned by God to do the good works which He planned before time began. I am His co-laborer. I have nothing to fear and everything to look forward to.

REFLECTION:

_____
_____
_____
_____
_____
_____
_____
_____
_____
_____
_____
_____
_____

PART FOUR
MOVING FORWARD

We have remembered who God is, recognized who we are, and refreshed our relationship with Him. It is time to move forward in our spiritual quest: the desire to know Him and interact with Him on a more intimate and deeper level than ever before. Here is where the rubber meets the road. Here is what we have been waiting for, longing for, and thirsting for—the action steps to achieve this life.

DAY 24
STEP 1: RESPOND

God has given you a commission that is personally yours . . . it is yours and yours alone. No one else can fill your shoes. No one else can walk your path. No one else can be you. With that knowledge and understanding, the next step is simply to *respond.*

Respond to the God of the Universe, who laid out this purpose and plan for you. Respond by agreeing to step out into that plan and purpose. Respond by trusting Him in this season of your life.

Walk out your commission expectantly—in faith, believing that He will do what He has said. He always keeps His promises—on that you can rely. It is His character and who He is. He does not and cannot change. He is God.

Agree with Him. After all, He is the all-powerful, all-knowing, and ever-present God. And if you don't agree with

Him? Well, have that conversation with Him also. See what He says about it. Listen . . . Hear . . . Consider . . . Then decide. Will you or will you not follow His lead?

If your answer is no, and you choose not to follow Him, you may want to stop here in this book. Why? Because everything that lies ahead hinges on this one decision.

If you find you are not ready to agree with Him today, do not completely walk away. Give yourself some time to really think about it. Put this book down until you are ready to take the next step. He is patient and loves you enough to wait for you.

Contemplation: What does it look like for you to respond to His call? Are you ready?

Prayer: Lord, show me how to respond today. If my heart is not ready, please work on that part of me.

Psalm 27:8 NLT

My heart has heard you say, "Come and talk with me." And my heart responds, "Lord, I am coming."

DECLARATION

My reflection on the call that He has given me will be directed by Him, not by me. I will not rush the process. He will be my guide, bringing to mind memories, spiritual markers, and words spoken to and over me. He will clarify my past and will direct my future.
He will show me the next step.

REFLECTION:

DAY 25
STEP 2: RENEW

Just as winter leads to spring and new life, acceptance of our individual commission brings a need for new focus. After revealing our purpose to us, God wants to renew us so that we can maximize our effectiveness in the calling He has before us.

For this day, we will focus on the renewal of our heart, mind, and commitment to the Lord.

Offer your heart anew to the Savior. Ask Him to reveal anything that needs cleansing, anything that needs healing. Is there any part of your heart that you are holding back from Him?

You can trust Him completely with your heart. People are fallible, but God is infallible. He will never let you down or betray your trust.

Remember how much He loves you? His perfect love provides the emotional safety you long for. He wants what is BEST for you, so let Him show you what needs to be renewed. Let Him show you what needs to be surrendered.

How do you renew your mind? First, you must ask Him to give you the mind of Christ. He wants you to surrender to being ruled by the Spirit, but that decision is yours. You must ask for it and pursue it. Renew your mind so that your thoughts and desires will honor and glorify Him.

Of course you won't be perfect! Having the mind of Christ is a work in progress. Because we live in a fallen world and we are sinners by nature, even when we do our best every day, we will always have challenges. We are exposed to things in our culture that are contrary to the character and will of God. We must be aware that renewing our minds is a daily challenge.

Renewing our mind is not primarily about being able to carry out our purpose.

The primary reason to renew our minds is to maintain the intimacy of our relationship with God, which is what *really* matters. Everything else flows from that relationship. When our relationship with God is intimate, the "everything else" seems almost effortless—it is such a good place to be . . .

Renew your commitment to Him today. Take a moment to remind yourself and to tell Him that you are committed—committed to your relationship with Him, committed to the purpose He has set before you, and committed to seeking a life of intimacy with Him.

Remember, none of this is about performance. It is about relationship.

Contemplation: Think about what it means to be committed to a relationship with God. How does that look for you? What would it mean in your life?

Prayer: Lord, give me the desire to seek the renewing of my mind to become more like You. Transform me by Your grace.

Romans 12:2 NIV

Do not conform to the pattern of this world, but be transformed by the renewing of your mind.

DECLARATION

I declare a renewal of my heart and mind today, and every day, as He draws me into a closer relationship. Transformation is His work in me.

REFLECTION:

DAY 26
STEP 3: RELINQUISH

Hand it over. Whatever it is that you are trying to control, hand it over to Him.

Relinquish it *all* to Him.

Ask Him in this moment to show you what it is that you need to turn over to Him.

Take a few moments and be still in His presence. Sit quietly and listen, calming your mind so you can hear the Father speak. This may take a little practice, but you can do it. Ask the Father to speak to you through the Spirit.

If you cannot hear right now, don't worry. Ask Him to speak to you today and He will, but you must have your spiritual ears open and be anticipating that He will answer.

If something was revealed to you immediately, you might want to discuss this with the Father. There may be something that you are trying to control that He wants you to turn over to Him. What does the need to be in control say about you and your level of trust in Him? Are there past injuries or fears that need to be worked through?

Let Him reveal what He wants to reveal. Don't try to figure it out all by yourself.

It's like peeling the layers of an onion. As He reveals and you relinquish control of certain areas of your life, you will continue to see other areas that need to be relinquished to Him.

Trust Him. He is faithful, and you can count on Him.

Contemplation: What are the benefits of giving the control back to God?

Prayer: Lord, show me one thing I need to trust you with today.

Proverbs 3:5–6 NIV

Trust in the Lord with all your heart and lean not on your own understanding. In all your ways submit to him, and he will make your paths straight.

DECLARATION

I declare that I have complete trust in the Father. I willingly give Him control of every area He reveals to me. He has all the knowledge and power to guide me in the best direction concerning all aspects of my life. Even when I do not understand, I will trust Him.

REFLECTION:

_____
_____
_____
_____
_____
_____
_____
_____
_____
_____
_____
_____
_____
_____

DAY 27
STEP 4: REMEMBER

Here is the sweet spot—a return to the core of the relationship.

Take time today to remember your identity as a child of the Living God. Review section two of this book, and your responses to each day.

Then recall your spiritual markers—those incidents and people in your life that all worked together to get you to where you are today. As you review those markers, take time to marvel at God's hand in it all, and thank Him. Express your gratitude to Him aloud or in writing. Acknowledge Him and His role in your life.

Focus for a few moments on the time when you came to know Jesus as your Savior, when you asked Him into your heart and life. Remember the love and passion you felt in that moment. If it is not a vivid memory, ask Him to recall a moment when you were passionate about Him and about your faith. Then sit in that for a few moments, experiencing it once again.

Finally, remember your God-given purpose. Remember what He spoke to you about your purpose in Him. Recall that it is yours and yours alone—that it was specially designed for you before time began. Rest in the knowledge that He who started a good work in you will be faithful to complete it.

Today is a day of remembrance.

Contemplation: Memory is a mighty tool, bringing us full circle to where we started and showing how we got to where we are today. How can you harvest those memories for good, and for the renewing of your mind? Perhaps you will see them in a different light at this stage of your walk with Him.

Prayer: Lord, bring to mind all of the spiritual markers You have placed throughout my life, that I may remember You and Your good works on my behalf. May You be praised and glorified through my remembrance.

Revelation 3:3 NIV

Remember therefore, what you have received and heard; hold it fast, and repent.

DECLARATION

I declare that the work of the Lord is visible throughout my life. I will recall His goodness and I will be reminded of His faithfulness to me. He will bring to remembrance those moments as I reconnect with Him. The Lord is good, and His mercy endures forever.

REFLECTION:

DAY 28
STEP 5: RELEASE

Release your past. If you must revisit it to find closure, please do so. As you look at your past, ask God to help you see it through His eyes. Please do not attribute any feelings of shame or disappointment to God. Those only belong to you.

God cannot be disappointed because He is not surprised by anything. He already knows it all. Disappointment can only come if one is expecting something different from what happens.

And shame? He does not heap that on us. Shame is man-made and used by the evil one to hinder our progress.

Revisit your past if you must. Heal, if possible, but do not live there. Let the past stay in the past. You may acknowledge the effect your past has on you, but do not be a victim to it and do not let it control you. Your past does not define you, for you are not your past, so do not give any power to it.

Release those things in your past that hold you captive. Take those giants to the King and ask Him to cut off their heads. Once David cut off Goliath's head, Goliath no longer held any power over the people. This lesson was brought home to me by Jana Spicka at a women's retreat in September 2019. She taught this lesson, and then instructed us to ask God to show us what giants needed to be brought to Him.

I took that giant to God, and He cut the head right off. It no longer has any power over me. I cannot even bring it to mind any longer, even when I have tried. I thank God that He is faithful to reveal and faithful to heal.

Release your past today. In doing so, you bring yourself the freedom to walk boldly into your future.

Contemplation: Ask God what is one thing He wants you to release today?

Prayer: Lord, make Your voice clear—so clear that I cannot possibly deny it is from You. Give me the desire and resolve to release whatever You show me from my past into Your hands.

Philippians 3:13–14 NIV

Brothers and sisters, I do not consider myself yet to have taken hold of it. But one thing I do know: **Forgetting what is behind** *and straining to what is ahead, I press on toward the goal to win the prize for which God has called me heavenward in Christ Jesus.*

DECLARATION

I declare that all which has held me captive up to this point is released to God and to His care. I have found and willingly receive the freedom He so graciously gives to those who ask. I walk in the favor of the Lord God Almighty. His goodness and mercy will follow me all the days of my life.

REFLECTION:

DAY 29
STEP 6: RESURRECT YOUR PASSION

Resurrect your passion for your walk with Him. God chose you. He made you and designed you. As part of that design, He created in you a passion. It is a God-given passion that should help direct your energies in this life.

As wounded humans, we are constantly seeking to fill the void created by our broken relationship with our Creator. While it is a void that only He can fill, we often attempt to fill it with so many other things. The things of this life are finite. Their beauty and appeal are passing.

But the things of God are timeless, infinite. They satiate our spiritual hunger and quench our thirsting spirit. I hope you have experienced a taste of these things God has to offer. If not, now is an opportunity to cultivate your taste, to whet your appetite, to sooth your thirsty soul.

Resurrect the passion you once felt for Him. Your passion may have only been a weak fire or it may have cooled as you became busier and busier in your life. Now is the time to spark the flame, to reignite what was once present, and to fuel it to a larger and hotter flame than before.

What has He called you to? What passion did He set inside of you that has been extinguished for some time now?

You know . . . deep in your heart you know, but maybe you cannot recall or cannot hear your heart speaking to you. Sit quietly with the Father, if not in body, then in spirit, and let Him remind you of the passion that once burned for Him and for His work.

Let Him Resurrect your passion . . .

Contemplation: What is your forgotten passion?

Prayer: Father, remind me. Peel the layers of myself away to reveal the passion You placed in my heart and soul.

Revelation 3:15 NIV

I know your deeds, that you are neither hot nor cold. I wish you were either one or the other!

DECLARATION

I declare that my God-given passion is part of who I am. Though it may be hidden or diminished at the present time, it will burn brightly again. God will bring it to life and will guide me in my steps to live out what He placed inside of me. It is my purpose. My passion begins and ends with Him.

REFLECTION:

DAY 30
STEP 7: RECREATE YOUR FUTURE

The future is just that—the future. It is not certain. It is not cut in stone. It is not laid out in a fixed plan.

Your future is yours to create, or rather, to recreate.

Why do I use the word "recreate?" Because everything you have done up to this point has led you in a particular direction, but *you* can change the direction of your future by making *different choices* in your life. By changing your *focus* and your *mindset*. You may not be able to change your current circumstances, but you can change how your mind perceives and acts on them.

Let your mind focus on Him—the God of the Universe. As you continue in a more intimate walk with Him, He will begin to reveal even more of Himself to you.

As HE reveals, begin to write it down. (Habakkuk 2:2)

GOD is faithful. He keeps His word, and He has a plan for you. He will reveal it if you ask and listen. Set yourself and the things of this world aside—choose Him and His plan.

As He begins to reveal your purpose and His plan, you will have one of two responses. You will either joyfully jump into the plan and embrace it with everything in you, or find every reason it cannot possibly happen.

Unfortunately, most of us will respond in the second way.

There are a multitude of reasons we hesitate to follow God including fear of failure, fear of what we may have to give up, and fear of the opinions of others. Maybe we are comfortable with our lives the way they are and don't want to risk changing our status quo.

There are many "what ifs" when we make a choice to change.

The truth is that change comes whether we choose it or not. Since this is a truth of life, I will choose to change with Him.

I choose to face my future and recreate it with His guidance and His help.

You see, when God calls us out, we are never alone. HE is always with us. I once heard someone explain it as always having a small group of three with you: the Father, the Son, and the Holy Spirit. You are never alone, and He will place others in your life to help you or to walk the journey with you.

You just have to trust Him.

Recreate your future. Cultivate your relationship with your Creator. Hear Him clearly and follow His lead. You can never go wrong doing this.

Contemplation: The future looks entirely different when molded by the hands of the Creator God. How is it different for you? What dream has He placed in your heart that He wants to fulfill?

Prayer: Lord, help me to get out of Your way so that my future can be all You intended it to be. Help me trust that You are leading me every step of the way. Keep me from limiting You by trying to control what Your plan looks like for me.

John 20:21 NIV

Again Jesus said, "Peace be with you! As the Father has sent me, I am sending you."

DECLARATION

I declare that my future is known and is under the direction of the Lord God Almighty. I surrender my future to His most capable hands. I will listen and follow His lead as we recreate my future together.

REFLECTION:

_____
_____
_____
_____
_____
_____
_____
_____
_____
_____
_____
_____
_____

DAY 31
STEP 8: RELISH THE RELATIONSHIP

The time has come to simply enjoy this relationship with the Creator of the Universe. You have revisited key aspects of God's character and your standing with Him. You have explored the steps of being relational with Him.

Hopefully by this time, you have found a renewed passion and a desire for a deeper intimacy with God, and you are working toward that daily.

In the quiet moments with Him, you have learned to hear His voice, to understand His heart, and to recognize when your Shepherd calls to you.

You have experienced His presence, felt His love, and known His goodness toward you.

Take these moments today to sit in contentment with Him and with your relationship.

While there will always be questions, corrections, and frustrations throughout your walk along this path of life, you may rest in the assurance of His unending love and care for you, and in His desire to have a close relationship with you—every moment of the day.

Today, just enjoy it, taking great pleasure in it as you go through your day. Marvel in the knowledge that this is unending and that He will always desire your heartfelt seeking of Him.

Make your relationship with Him your number one priority, seeking Him above all. Know that He rewards those who diligently seek Him.

Rest in the love of the Father for you, His child. And just as a small child, content in the arms of their parent, be secure in the knowledge that He is ever-present, ever-watchful, and ever-available for you.

Relish your unique relationship with your God.

Contemplation: Your Father loves to spend time with you. Today, just think about how much He enjoys being with you.

Prayer: Lord, let me know Your presence. Let me be covered in Your Spirit. Let me find great delight in Your company, today and each day as we walk together.

Psalm 37:4 NIV

Take delight the Lord, and He will give you the desires of your heart.

DECLARATION

I declare that my greatest joy is found in my relationship with my Heavenly Father. I will intentionally seek Him. I will soak in His love and care. We will walk together as Father and child, as friends. I will delight in being with Him as He delights in being with me.

REFLECTION:

AFTERWORD

As I worked through this writing, I had no idea where I would end up, or what He would be changing and doing in my life. This year, I have indeed changed. My future rests in his hands, and I am secure in it, whatever it holds.

My faith has been reignited, my passion has been clarified, and my heart is stronger toward Him. I long for my brothers and sisters in Christ to experience Him as I have! But I also know that everyone is on their own spiritual journey, and that each road is different.

I pray that in some way this book has touched you and has moved you along that path toward knowing Him more intimately. It is the sweetest place to be.

Whatever you do, **don't stop here**. Don't stop seeking Him. Don't stop thirsting after Him. I echo the psalmist in my prayer for you, that as the deer pants for the water, your soul will long for God. That a deepening relationship with Him will be your all-encompassing desire.

Dig into the Word. Spend time with Him. Communicate and commune with Him. Delight yourself in Him and He will give you the desires of your heart (Psalms 37:4, NIV).

Enjoy the journey.

Ann

Do you know Jesus as your Lord and Savior? This book assumes you have a personal relationship with Him, but I would be remiss to leave the Gospel out of this message.

Jesus came to this earth as a man, the son of God, born to a virgin. He lived a sinless life and became the final and complete sacrifice for the sins of all mankind. He died on a cross, was buried in a tomb, and rose again to life on the third day, just as He said He would. Many people bore witness to his bodily resurrection as He walked on earth for 40 days before He ascended to the Father.

Jesus is the way, the truth, and the life. We come to the Father only through Him, by accepting His gift of salvation.

The following scriptures are for your benefit. Read through them. Allow God to speak to your heart. If you do not know Him as your Lord and Savior, you have only to ask Him. He is faithful and trustworthy.

For all have sinned and fall short of the glory of God. Romans 3:23

For the wages of sin is death, but the gift of God is eternal life in Christ Jesus our Lord. Romans 6:23

Jesus replied, "Very truly I tell you, no one can see the kingdom of God unless they are born again." John 3:3

Jesus answered, "I am the way, the truth and the life. No one comes to the Father except through me." John 14:6

If you declare with your mouth "Jesus is Lord" and believe in your heart that God raised him from the dead, you will be saved. For it is with your heart that you believe and

> *are justified, and it is with your mouth that you profess your faith and are saved.*
> *Romans 10:9–10*

> *Believe in the Lord Jesus and you will be saved.*
> *Acts 16:31*

If you have made a decision to become a follower of Christ, I urge you to tell someone. Become part of a fellowship of believers so that you may grow in community. Ask the Lord to lead you to the right people and the right place where you will be discipled in the truth of His word.

May God richly bless you as you journey forward with Him. *He who began a good work in you will carry it on to completion. Philippians 1:6 NIV*

Made in the USA
Monee, IL
07 June 2022